Dodge CHALLENGER
& Plymouth BARRACUDA

David Newhardt

MBI Publishing Company

Dedication

To my mother, Lois L. Newhardt, who encouraged
me to pursue my dreams, no matter how crazy.

First published in 2000 by MBI Publishing Company, 729
Prospect Avenue, PO Box 1, Osceola, WI 54020-0001 USA

MBI Publishing Company books are also available at
discounts in bulk quantity for industrial or sales-promotional
use. For details write to Special Sales Manager at
Motorbooks International Wholesalers & Distributors,
729 Prospect Avenue, PO Box 1, Osceola, WI 54020-0001
USA.

Library of Congress Cataloging-in-Publication Data Available

ISBN 0-7603-0772-5

On the front cover: The 1971 Hemi 'Cuda and the 1970
Dodge Challenger T/A are two of the finest Chrysler musclecars
ever produced. The Hemi 'Cuda is equipped with the legendary
425-horsepower 426-ci firebreather. The Challenger T/A carries
the high-revving 275-horsepower 340 V-8.

On the frontispiece: The shaker hood intake belongs to one
of two Panther Pink 1970 Hemi 'Cudas built. Underneath the
ram air intake resides the venerable 426-ci Hemi.

On the title page: The 1974 Plymouth 'Cuda is the last of a
proud breed. During its four year life span, the E-body grew
longer and heavier. With a 360 under the hood, the 'Cuda
pumped out 245 net horsepower. The trim lines remained
intact in 1974. A simple grille design resided between the
single headlights. The air inlets on the hood were for show
only, but they were still good looking.

On the back cover: This 1969 'Cuda had little room to spare
in the engine bay when the 440-ci V-8 was stuffed inside.
Drivers had 375 horsepower on tap at 4,600 rpm. With such
a large engine over the front wheels, it didn't handle like a
Ford Boss 302, but for straightline thrust, there were only a
few cars that could beat it.

Edited by Paul Johnson
Designed by Doug Tiedman

Printed in China

CONTENTS

ACKNOWLEDGMENTS

Many thanks to the owners that allowed me to photograph their wonderful vehicles: Dan and Paula Smith, Ken Soto, Walter Grant, Sue DiMaio, Dick Roche, Bob Gough, Brit White, Cliff and Lynn Cunningham, Keith Stone, Ken Benedict, Kenn Funk, Paul Orlowski, Tom Parker, Rodney Kneece, Rick Shelar, Doug Coull, Jeff Paschal, Michael Carter, Alan Prokop, Donny Dotson, Julius Steuer, Jack Berdasko, Kris Tadey, Norm and Lloyd Ver Hage, Harold Sullivan, Charlie Miller, Kim Newhouse, Otis Chandler, and Scott Harvey.

Thanks to the following for their valuable contributions: Robert Genat, Randy Leffingwell, John Herlitz, Sjoerd Dijkstra, David Hakim, Mike Jones, Matt Stone, Bob Riggle, Milt Antonick, Brian Tracy of the NHRA, Tom Krefetz, Sam Posey, and The Mopar Club of San Diego. Special thanks to my long-suffering sons, Branden and Ryan, my lady Susan Foxx, and my editor Paul Johnson.

INTRODUCTION

Mopar or no car! I heard this quite a bit while writing this book. I came to understand the reason for this kind of loyalty-pulling for the underdog. The story of the Plymouth Barracuda and Dodge Challenger show how the pendulum can swing in Detroit. Originally conceived as a sport derivative of the Valiant, the Barracuda was targeted toward the youth market, but it was too closely allied with the compact car for far too long. It was not able to shake the stigma of "economy car" until 1970, when an all-new E-body style made its debut. In the years before the E-body saw the showroom, the Barracuda was developed and honed to a fine road car, capable of holding its own against the best from domestic manufacturers. Unfortunately, the market was not kind to the Chrysler Pony Car. For many years, the Ford Mustang outsold the Barracuda 10 to 1. Was the Mustang 10 times the car? Of course not. But Ford knew how to market what it had. And it did not waste time developing new products. This was the biggest problem for Chrysler, having a showroom full of old products. The E-bodies would have seen impressive sales if only they had been introduced two years earlier.

Of course, if everyone had a crystal ball, no one would make mistakes. Failing that, engineers make educated guesses, and companies live and die with the consequences. We can all say that this or that should have been done. But one thing is certain: Chrysler built one of the most exciting pony cars of the entire era. Properly equipped, it could outperform all but a handful of other cars. Yet such performance was available to anyone who walked into a showroom with a fistful of money. That vehicles like these, capable of truly incredible performance, actually became a production item is all the more astonishing. We will never see their kind again. Long live the Mopars!

CHAPTER 1
THE HIGH-PERFORMANCE VALIANT
BARRACUDA 1964–1966

Pontiac had introduced its LeMans GTO in 1964, showing that it was changing its image. It was also a glimpse into the future. Soon after the GTO was released, Ford sprang the Mustang on America. When the year was over, about 500,000 Mustangs had been sold, and a new market niche, the high-performance youth market, had been created. In a few short years, Detroit's Big Three would be churning out high-powered V-8 musclecars. The Chrysler Corporation had learned that Ford was developing the Mustang, a new model targeted to the youth market, before it was released. So the push was on at Chrysler to get a comparable vehicle designed as quickly and economically as possible. At the time, there was no intention of producing what would eventually be called a musclecar.

The Plymouth Valiant was chosen as the donor platform to take on the new Ford Mustang. Designer Irv Ritchie and studio manager Dave Cummins developed the idea of a wraparound

backlight on the Valiant in 1959. By late 1962, clay renderings of the car showed how the standard Valiant Signet 200 series lines were intact, with the exception of the roof section and the grilles. When the push from Chrysler headquarters for a youth model heated up, Cummins' designs were put into metal. Designer Milt Antonick recalls that funds for a lavish design just weren't in the cards. "We wanted to do more. We wanted to put a new shell on it. And we got it for 1967. But for the first Barracuda, tooling costs were a very, very minimal thing. Everything was on a shoestring. Sales results were closely watched, even in the design department. A few bad weeks in showrooms would lead directly to companywide staffing cuts." On April 1, 1964, the new high-performance Valiant was introduced as the Plymouth Valiant Barracuda. The Barracuda's first incarnation was not a glorious statement of Chrysler musclecar performance. From humble beginnings, however, the

Essentially a 1964 Plymouth Valiant with a fastback grafted onto it, the 1964 Barracuda was assembled on the same production line as the Valiant. Engines offered were a base 101-horsepower 170-ci slant six, a larger 225-ci, 145-horsepower six, and the new 180-horsepower 273-ci V-8 grille.

The taillight of the first year Barracuda was lifted directly from the Valiant. The backup lights and rear bumper guards were optional. This taillight treatment changed little until the second-generation Barracuda was introduced in 1967.

Barracuda evolved into one of the truly outstanding musclecars of the era. And it would be one of the best and fastest musclecars to roll off the Chrysler assembly lines. In turn, it left its distinct mark on the automotive landscape.

The base 101-horsepower, 170-ci "slant six" engine didn't provide sterling performance by any stretch of the imagination, but fitted with an optional small-block V-8, it provided competent performance. By increasing the stroke, the 170-ci displacement was increased to 225 ci with a power increase to 145 horsepower. If a six was not enough, the 273-ci V-8 mill with 8.8:1 compression ratio and two-barrel carburetor was the only option. It kicked out a whopping 180 horsepower and 260 foot-pounds.

Only 16 days after the Barracuda hit the street, Ford introduced the soon-to-be-legendary Mustang. It, too, was equipped with a base six-cylinder engine, putting out 101 horsepower, but the optional 289-ci V-8 produced 271 horsepower. Much like the Barracuda, the Mustang was based off an existing Ford platform (the Falcon); however, it had all-new sheet metal and no obvious ties to its past.

The first year Barracuda had a plush, comfortable interior, torsion-bar front suspension, two outboard-mounted asymmetrical leaf springs in the rear, and the excellent TorqueFlite automatic transmission. With a wheelbase of 106 inches, the Barracuda was a compact, but due to its torsion-bar front suspension, ride quality was impressively smooth and handling was comparatively better than the Mustang. Ten-inch drum brakes all on corners provided adequate braking prowess.

With the exception of a minor grille change, the Barracuda was a standard Valiant from the firewall forward. The "greenhouse," or the rear window or fastback roof design, was the distinguishing

The interior of the first generation Barracuda was pure 1960s. The 1964 model was the only year that used push buttons for the optional TorqueFlite automatic transmission. Period brochures pointed out that the "Wood-grained steering wheel gives you the feel of a 'racing car.'" Transistorized push-button AM radio was a strong selling feature.

visual change from the Valiant. The fastback design helped to visually balance the car, which, when compared to the new Mustangs' long hood-short deck style, was more conventional from a design standpoint. The addition of the vast, 2,070-square-inch rear window, at the time the largest single piece of glass ever installed in a passenger car, helped give the vehicle a handsome, rakish look. Under that expanse of glass,

the car had 23.7 square feet of luggage space when the rear seat was folded down. This was a typical midsized, mid-1960s American car, which meant that it was expected to carry five people and their luggage and look good doing it.

Front bucket seats, a folding rear seat, and a "security panel" that allowed access through the trunk into the interior were part of the appeal of the Barracuda. A sales brochure from 1964

The rear seating area could be transformed into a huge 23.7cubic-foot storage space simply by grasping the chromed catch bar and flipping the seatback forward. For additional room, the panel between the interior and the trunk could be lowered into the trunk, allowing objects up to 7 feet long to be stored in the security of a locked car. Note the abundance of chrome trim pieces around the carpet seams, and the chromed gas tank filler tube.

spoke glowingly of the vinyl-clad interiors that came in "glamorous gold, rich blue or black or bright red." The "simple, sporty lines" of the instrument panel gave the interior a "clean, fresh look." Bright trim adorned the cabin, and the doors shut with an authoritative sound.

Unlike the Mustang that was available in both coupe and convertible, the Barracuda was offered in a fastback model only. First year sales were promising and demonstrated the car had found a market, but it was far off the success of its rival, the Mustang. In the last four months of 1964, 23,443 Barracudas were sold, but Ford sold a whopping 126,538 Mustangs.

When *Car Life* magazine put a 273-ci V-8 Barracuda (described by the factory as "husky") through its paces, it came up with a 0-60 mile-per-hour time of 12.9 seconds and a top speed of 105 miles per hour, respectable times for the era and 180 horsepower power plant. A four-speed manual transmission with a Hurst shifter was one of the few "sporting" options available that

The front grille in 1966 allowed more air to reach the radiator, eliminating the cooling problems that plagued the first year-and-a-half models. In an attempt to distance the Barracuda from the Valiant, the swimming "fish" emblem made its debut in 1966, but on internal company records the vehicle was still referred to by the BV series designation.

year. But that would change, as Plymouth saw the pony car market heat up and big sales numbers in the Blue Oval.

Formula S Is Born

For 1965 the exterior of the Barracuda changed minimally, but it received a performance infusion. The Valiant name was shorn from the body, and the high-performance Formula S option first appeared. This was the beginning of a long line of wonderfully exciting musclecars from Chrysler. Chrysler engineer Scott Harvey, a road race and rally driver in his spare time, tested and developed suspension parts to create the

performance package. Racing is said to improve the breed, and the Formula S package is the perfect example. Harvey's racing experience with Valiants allowed him to pick the right spring rates and shock absorbers to give the Barracuda a more sporting feel. Because the Barracuda was slightly heavier than the Valiant, small changes were needed compensate for the weight. The steering gear was changed to a 16:1 ratio manual gear from 24:1 to quicken the steering response. Scott Harvey recounted, "We just reworked some power gears into a manual to get the right ratio." The Barracuda made other significant strides in the handling department, with

wide-rim 14-inch wheels and Goodyear Blue Streak tires, 6.95x14, and the Rallye Pack suspension consisting of "Firm-Ride" shock absorbers, six leaf springs rather than four, and a sway bar. Straight-line performance got a necessary shot in the arm with the introduction of the "Commando 273" V-8 engine. This power plant had 10.5:1 compression, a four-barrel carburetor, and dual exhaust, all of which significantly increased output. Engine internals included a high-lift/high-overlap camshaft, dome-shaped pistons, and a dual point distributor. An unsilenced air cleaner and dual exhaust helped the mill breathe and made the small-block sound absolutely glorious. Power front disc brakes were available as a dealer-installed option. The standard 273-ci engine produced 180 horsepower, which was good enough for a 0-60 miles-per-hour time of 10.5 seconds. It wasn't the kind of performance that was going to win many pick slips in straight-up races with the competition, but it was a definite improvement. The top-level engine put out 235 horsepower, and propelled *Motor Trend* staffers from 0-60 in 8 seconds flat and hit a top speed of 110 miles per hour, according to the magazine's January 1965 issue. A run down the quarter-mile was achieved in 16.1 seconds, flashing through the

If the upper part of the vehicle is covered, you could be excused for thinking that you were looking at a Plymouth Valiant. The Valiant badging is located inboard of the right-side taillight. *Chrysler*

Scott Harvey's family car.

Some family car! Scott's car, like most of those campaigned in serious sedan racing, has been specially modified to make it a little more race car and a little less street machine.

It's sort of interesting to note, though, that there are several things that didn't need changing to turn our Formula 'S' Barracuda into a SCCA National Champion. Like disc brakes. And the heavy-duty suspension. And the limited-slip differential. And the basics of our 273-cu.-in. V-8. And the fast-ratio steering gear . . . all of these standard or available on the production Formula 'S'.

And so are a few other items that make the 'S' a car that's perfect for the street, and that can still knock off an occasional rally or gymkhana. Front bucket seats, a rear seat that flips down into a seven-foot-long cargo space and slippery fastback styling.

Now with all of this, don't you think it might be more fun to win a rally with a family car? Talk to your Plymouth Dealer right away and see.

PLYMOUTH DIVISION  **CHRYSLER** MOTORS CORPORATION

Plymouth ...a great car by Chrysler Corporation.

finish line lights at 87 miles per hour. This was an admirable time from a car that carried around 3,170 pounds.

During this time, Chrysler Corporation was recognized for its engineering excellence, and the Barracuda was a typically well-crafted piece. The heavy-duty torsion bar front suspension and stiffer rear springs supplied a smooth ride and respectable handling. The 108-inch wheelbase helped the Barracuda attain a nimble feel.

Road & Track magazine put a 1965 Barracuda Formula S through its paces and got similar performance results to the *Motor Trend* test: 0-60 miles per hour in 8.2 seconds and a quarter-mile run in 15.9 seconds at a blistering 85 miles per hour. But *R&T* wound up its report extolling the vehicle's practical virtues. "For those people who enjoy sports car driving but, for reasons of family or business, need four seats and adequate baggage space, the Barracuda would certainly make an excellent compromise."

Unfortunately, the public wanted stylish flash in the sporty car market. Plymouth originally had no intention of pursuing the market in the sports direction. But the Mustang dragged Chrysler into that market segment. As such, the Pentastar group was not immediately ready to fight for market share, so Ford cleaned up. Barracuda sales in model year 1965 were a respectful 64,596-the highest number this generation of Barracuda would achieve. In fact, the Barracuda posted the highest sales numbers in the entire Plymouth line. But compared with same year Mustang sales of 559,451, the gang at Plymouth had its work cut out to get on terms with the Mustang, at least as far as market acceptance was concerned.

A Slightly Evolved Barracuda

Model year 1966 was another year of incremental evolution for the Barracuda. Some minor rear-end styling changes and an imposing front end were the significant design changes. The Barracuda emblem, an aggressive profile of the salt-water predator styled by Milt Antonick, was unveiled. A new instrument panel was introduced, and shell-type bucket seats replaced those in the older design. Visitors to a Plymouth showroom had 17 colors to choose from on their Barracuda. The Formula S option was carried over, and front disc brakes were finally made available from the factory.

The interior underwent redesign. The Formula S package included a 150-mile-per-hour speedometer and a 6,000-rpm tachometer. The power plant went unchanged, so the upper range of that speedometer collected dust. Actually, many cars themselves collected dust because the dated styling hindered sales. While Barracuda sales plummeted by 42 percent to only 38,029 units, Ford cranked out 607,568 Mustangs in the same time frame. Chrysler was concerned, and another player was going to join the market shortly. One of the worst-held secrets was that a General Motors musclecar was preparing an entry in the super-hot pony car field. The event precipitated the design and development of the E-body chassis. But Plymouth was not giving up without a fight, and for 1967 its dealers had an improved weapon for fighting for market share.

In an attempt to capitalize on the dramatic racing results that Chrysler engineer Scott Harvey was earning at the wheel of a Barracuda, his family was enlisted to pose with his race car. Harvey's modifications were the basis for the Formula S package that injected performance into the Barracuda. Writing for *Sports Car Graphic* in March 1966, racer Jerry Titus called the Formula S the "Most roadable production four-seater Detroit has ever made."

CHAPTER 2
A MORE MUSCULAR FISH
BARRACUDA 1967–1969

All new. The Barracuda was now designed to fight and outswim other rivals in the musclecar pond. The first-generation fish didn't break new ground in technology, styling, or performance, but the new car's foray into the burgeoning musclecar youth market met with some success. A larger part of the target audience considered it to be little more than a warmed-over Plymouth Valiant, and to a large degree it was a Valiant. The Ford Mustang was making automotive history and setting sales records for Ford. And Chevrolet answered the call by introducing Camaro for 1967. Chrysler had to step up to the plate and release a genuine musclecar if it was going stay competitive with its rival manufacturers.

Horsepower and Dimensions on the Rise

On November 26, 1966, three new A-body styles were introduced for Plymouth's 1967 model year: a fastback, a notchback coupe, and a convertible. If the model variation worked for the Mustang, it should work for the fish! Milt Antonick recalls that "the decision makers at Chrysler were finally aware that the product (Barracuda) was going to be around for a while. But before they were going to put a dime into the platform, they wanted to be sure that it would succeed. The sales of the Mustang helped the Barracuda."

Chrysler followed Detroit's trend of increased body dimensions and stretched the wheelbase to 108 inches, while the overall length expanded more than 4 inches, to 192.8 inches. But the Pentastar group demonstrated that it was serious about high performance by expanding the width of the engine compartment by 2

The second-generation Barracuda was introduced with the race-derived Formula S package already on the option list. The pony car gained some serious legs with the installation of the 383-ci engine. Due to the large size of the block, air conditioning, power steering, and power brakes were mandatory deletes. The car posted quarter-mile times in the mid-14-second range at about 97 miles per hour. Only 1,841 383-equipped Formula S Barracudas rolled out of dealerships in 1967.

The 1969 Barracuda was available in one of three available body styles. Besides the fastback and coupe, the convertible was a very stylish option. When equipped with the 340-ci engine, the Formula S package was one of the best-handling setups on any pony car of the era. The power-operated top was fitted with a glass rear window, thus avoiding the dreaded fogged Plexiglas opacity.

inches. As we will see, this room was essential for ultimate high-performance goals.

The Plymouth design team did a masterful job revamping the second-generation Barracuda. For the first time, the new 'Cuda was visually separated from its past. Three choices were presented for the second-generation Chrysler pony car. The first was to build the Barracuda along the same lines as the first generation, using the new Valiant as the basis, and incorporating minor changes. The second option was to cover the Valiant underbody and windshield with all-new sheet metal. The third possibility was to design an all-new car, capable of fitting any size engine under the hood.

The final second-generation Barracuda took the middle road, as John Herlitz later described.

"They took the design elements that I had developed on the all-new car and as best possible, Dave Cummins, studio manager, crafted that design onto the A-body underbody," Herlitz recalled. A good dose of "European" flavor found its way into the fender lines and curves of the Pentastar pony car. The split grille, a Barracuda trademark since the vehicle was introduced, was retained and updated. A security door between the trunk and the passenger compartment was still offered. In conjunction with the folding rear seatback, items of up to 7 feet in length could be stored inside the vehicle. The notchback coupe had a graceful rear window, with a gentle Vee, before the large trunk lid swept into the clean, concave rear light treatment. And the convertible boasted a power top

The fitting of the 383-ci engine cost the Barracuda a small amount of handling prowess, but this option was designed for straight-line action. The attractive wheel covers were standard on the Formula S, and the mandatory front disc brakes were a useful addition. Sixty miles per hour would come up on the speedometer in as little as 7.4 seconds.

and a glass rear window, sparing the owner the embarrassment of a cloudy Plexiglas backlight. A quick-fill style gas cap was used, giving the car a more sporty look.

The interior was not ignored when the stylists turned their attention to the Barracuda. Bucket seats were standard with the convertible and optional in the vinyl and hardtop cars. Aluminum and pebble grain abounded, and the car had easy-to-read gauges in front of the driver. The buyer of the Interior Decor Group option got genuine simulated wood-grained trim, map pouches, and special upholstery, which hinted strongly at the Continental flavor. When bucket seats were installed, a center console was optional, and the result was a handsome cabin, fit for long-distance travels. With ample leg- and head-room, these

cars provided excellent ergonomics for a variety of body sizes.

It was hoped that visitors to Plymouth showrooms would ante up for the more expensive car. A base fastback went for $2,270 and the ragtop sold for $2,860.

V-8 Propulsion

Plymouth realized that power helped sell cars. While the base engine was the 145 horsepower 225-ci slant six, a pair of "A" engine small-block V-8s provided more inspiring performance. Although both engines displaced 273 cubes, the horsepower differences were considerable. The 180-horsepower version had an 8.8:1 compression ratio and breathed through a two-barrel carburetor. The hotter Commando

version had a 10.3:1 compression, a Carter four-barrel carb, and listed 235 horsepower output. If this was not enough oomph, the 383-ci mill could be selected from the option list. Ford had installed the 390-ci engine into the Mustang, so Plymouth, not to be left behind, shoehorned the big-block 383 V-8 into the Barracuda. The only way to get this power plant was to order the Formula S option, and the "B" engine Commando 383 big-block was a tight fit in the confines of the Barracuda's engine bay. The additional 2 inches in engine compartment width were dutifully used, and there wasn't any room to spare. Air conditioning, power steering, and power brakes were not available with the 383. There was just no room for these components! The engine's kinetic energy went to turn the rear tires rather than the components. The 383 had a compression ratio of 10.25:1 and a four-barrel carburetor, and a listed output of 280 horsepower at 4,200 rpm. This was down from the normal 325 horsepower due to the restrictive exhaust system imposed by the tight quarters of the engine compartment. But torque was rated at 400 foot-pounds at 2,400 rpm, and more than enough to tear a set of Red Streak D70x14 rear tires to shreds.

The superlative TorqueFlite automatic transmission or the durable A-833 four-speed manual transmission transmitted the horsepower to the rear axle. Chrysler offered a wide selection of options for the rear axle as well. If a buyer bought the 273 Commando engine bolted to an automatic transmission, the gearset ratio was a 3.23:1 with a 7-inch-diameter ring gear. The same ratio was standard with the 383

About all there was room for in the engine compartment was the engine when the 383-ci "B" mill was checked on the option list. Slipped into the 1967 Barracuda, the 383 engine produced 280 horsepower, which the following year increased to 300 horsepower. In 1969 it went higher yet, kicking out 330 horsepower.

From its drop-top to its Redlines, the 1968 Barracuda 340 Formula S was a head turner. And with its torsion bar front suspension, it handled as well as it looked. The simulated hood vents were an ideal location to highlight the engine displacement. The tonneau cover was held on with snaps with the top down and it lay in the roof well when the top was up.

Rare. Only 83 Barracuda 340-S convertibles were sold in 1969, and this one is fitted with the optional W23 cast-aluminum wheels, which makes it particularly rare. Fitted on vehicles for only two weeks, they had an annoying habit of loosening the lug nuts and detaching themselves from the car while in motion. Chrysler attempted to reclaim all the errant wheels to avoid any litigation. Only a few wheels currently exist and are very pricey.

engine. For a few dollars more, the optional 3.55:1 or 3.9:1 Sure-Grip ratios could be installed behind the 273 mill. The 383 engine did not come with any optional gearing from the factory, but a dealer could install a wide range of gear ratios, the better to satisfy the needs of individual buyers.

The suspension was little different from the first-generation Barracuda. Equipped with front torsion bars and rear leaf springs, it possessed handling characteristics superior to its pony car brethren. Drum brakes were still filling the wheels, unless a buyer checked the box for the optional front disc brakes. A 383 Formula S carried standard front disc brakes for obvious reasons.

But the focus of the Barracuda Formula S package was straight-line acceleration. With

From 1967 to 1969, the coupe featured a concave rear window and a concave rear taillight. The thin, graceful C-pillars instilled a lithe, well-proportioned balance to the Mopar pony car. This 383-equipped Formula S model was a purpose-built stoplight terror.

the 383 engine pushed to its limit, the Barracuda ran down the quarter-mile in the mid-14-second range and tripped the lights with a 97-mile-per-hour run. It produced a 0-60 time of 7.4 seconds. This was in line with its musclecar peers, but the push was on for yet more power and faster vehicles. This would become evident in the 1968 model year.

Refining the 'Cuda

With model year 1967 sales of 62,534 units, the Barracuda was not exactly on top of the sales chart. The competition was growing, and more was better. The competition pushed Chrysler to engineer better products, to do more with less. The 273 engine was retired in favor of the 318-ci V-8 base mill. And under the front expanse of metal was found a new power plant, the 340-ci small block became the standard engine for the Formula S. This small-block wonder produced a factory-claimed 275 horsepower at 5,000 rpm and 340 foot-pounds of torque at 3,200 revs. This engine was built to spin at high rpm and featured high-flow heads and huge 2.02-inch intake valves, which allowed the

Loaded with optional interior goodies, this 1967 Formula S was decked out with headrests, full-ring steering wheel, center console, an automatic transmission, and dealer installed air conditioning. The vivid copper interior was a glorious 1960s statement, a real treat for the eyes. Upscale appearances were maintained with a simulated burl dash.

Not a car for the faint of heart, the 1969 440 'Cuda was a brutal, straight-line beast. The distinctive hood stripes led back to a pair of nonfunctional hood scoops, and the dog-dish hubcaps were a quick tip-off that the driver put more stock in acceleration than appearance. Torque was listed at 480 foot-pounds at 3,200 rpm, more than sufficient to turn the Redlines into long black streaks.

engine to crank out impressive performance. A Carter AVS four-barrel carburetor resided on top of the dual-plane intake manifold. With a weight of 539 pounds, the car showed improved handling compared to 383-equipped Barracudas. Buyers of the Formula S option would get identifying simulated hood scoops broadcasting which power plant was lurking inside, either a 340-S or 383-S.

In the January 1968 issue of *Motor Trend*, a comparison test of a 340-equipped Barracuda against its competition showed that the fish was swimming near the head of the school. Pitted against a trio of big-block pony cars, a 396-ci Camaro, a 400-ci Ram Air II Firebird, and a 390-ci Mustang, the Barracuda posted a time of 15.2/92 miles per hour, almost identical to the three foes. Only a 343-ci Javelin beat it with a 15.1/93 mile per hour run, not exactly the stuff of a clean kill. A score of differing conditions on any given day could put the numbers in favor of the fish.

In the December 1967 issue of *Car Life*, a Barracuda 340-S was run through the wringer, leaving the editors duly impressed with the Plymouth pony car. "In the Barracuda 340-S, the driver can enjoy an exceptional car in many ways, an adequate car in nearly all ways, and a real value in the field of high-performance automobiles," they wrote. The performance was impressive, with a 0-60 mile-per-hour time of 7.0 seconds, while the quarter-mile was covered in 14.97 seconds at 95.4 miles per hour. Handling prowess was noted and lauded. "The Barracuda, while not a sports car, negotiated many curves at speeds that would give some accepted 'sports cars' considerable strain. The driver soon gets the feeling that it would take some incredible occurrence to make the Barracuda lose its grip on the pavement."

But as in the preceding year, the brunt of the Barracuda's reason for being was acceleration. Slowing the car down was still a partial act of

Literally shoehorned into the engine bay of a 1969 Barracuda, the Super Commando 440-ci "B" big-block engine left no room for power accessories. Instead, the full brunt of the engine was directed into the driveline, where the 375 horsepower came into their own at 4,600 rpm. With such a large engine over the front wheels, the lack of power steering meant that a lot of muscle was required for steering at slow speeds.

faith; drum brakes were the standard install unless the Formula S 383 was ordered. Front disc brakes were an option, but most buyers put their money under the hood.

Of course, the big block was still around, the 383-ci engine now boasting 300 horsepower to 4,200 rpm. Plymouth was getting serious about power generation, using technical specifications in advertisements. However, how many potential buyers were interested in valve overlap? Buyers wanted high performance-amazing acceleration and impressive top speed. These were built to hold their own, a quarter-mile at a time. And for those buyers who just had to be faster than everyone else, Plymouth offered a limited production Barracuda, one that would preface glory days to come.

Super Stock Super Fish

The 426-ci Hemi engine had seen street duty since late 1964. Few engines in automotive history are revered as much as the 426 Hemi. Rated at 425 horsepower in street trim, this big-block monster pumped out about 500 horsepower. In 1965 an exhibition drag racer *Hemi Under Glass* was built and campaigned. The vehicle was updated to second-generation bodywork in 1967 and continued its crowd-pleasing quarter-mile wheelstands. The positive response led Chrysler to stuff the 426 "Elephant" engine into the midsized Barracuda. The Hurst company, famous for its top-grade shifters, was enlisted to help build the ground pounders. When buyers ordered a Body Code BO29 Hemi Barracuda

The ultimate second-generation Barracuda was the marriage of the A-body with the famed Hemi engine in 1968. Built for sanctioned drag racing only, this vehicle required a new purchaser to sign a statement attesting to his or her knowledge that the Hemi Barracuda Super Stock was sold "as is." They didn't even come painted. Right out of a dealership, these vehicles could cover the quarter-mile in the mid-tens. Very rare, very brutal. *David Gooley*

The battery was in the trunk. It drank high-test like you owned a Sunoco station, and the only heater was the 426 Hemi living under the detachable fiberglass hood. With a pair of Holley carburetors atop a cross-ram intake manifold, the Hemi engine was barely able to fit between the front wheels. The master cylinder and right-side shock tower were moved to make room for the massive elephant engine, resulting in a vehicle weight of about 3,000 pounds. *David Gooley*

Super Stock, they were required to sign a letter stating that the vehicle was sold without a warranty, and that "The manufacturer assumes no responsibility for the manner in which such vehicles operate."

It was a very tight fit to install the Hemi into the engine bay. The engine had to be moved to the right 1 inch, and a special fiberglass hood was installed so the dual 1 11/16-inch Holley carburetors atop the Cross Ram dual manifold cleared the hood. The front fenders were made of the lightweight material as well, and the entire vehicle was lightened. Acid-dipped lightweight door skins were fitted to the car, and the conventional glass was replaced with Kemcore, a thin gauge (.080-inch), lightweight glass material. From the Hooker competition headers,

mechanical valve lifters, and transistor ignition, the car dripped with special competition equipment. It tipped the scales in the neighborhood of 3,000 pounds, and produced about 500 horsepower. These factory race cars were quick indeed, and they proved it in the SS/B and SS/BA classes. How does covering the quarter-mile in under 11 seconds and tripping the finish line lights at speeds in excess of 130 miles per hour sound? Ronnie Sox drove his Hemi to good effect in 1969, winning the Super Stock class at the 1969 spring Nationals with a run of 10.63 seconds, not bad for a car one could order from a dealer.

This was a one-year offering, and like many race models an exact build number is unknown. Estimates range between 50 and 70 units built.

The graceful, swimming Barracuda emblem was found on the front fenders of 1967 models. This symbol was one of the few things that carried over to the next generation of Barracudas, the E-bodies, in 1970.

The full-length racing stripe was an option that was intended to spice up the visual presence of the Barracuda, while the 383-ci Formula S package was depended on to deliver the goods. The attractive aluminum strip that ran the width of the rear was a clever styling aid. Designer Milt Antonick, a fan of imported sports cars, was responsible for the European-type filler cap.

The two-piece grille was a styling carryover from the first-generation Barracuda. This 1967 383 Formula S shows this successful design, unchanged during the entire three-year run. The 14-inch wheel covers were intended to convey the look of magnesium racing wheels without the high cost. The right-side mirror was a welcome option.

Graceful lines covered a brutish engine. The first year that the street slang name ('Cuda) was used by the factory was 1969. With a power-to-weight ratio that tended to favor straight-line acceleration, the 440 'Cuda was something of a wallowing pig when pushed in a corner. The 19.15:1 steering ratio guaranteed excitement when the tail would come around with throttle-induced oversteer.

But Plymouth forced everyone to sit up and take notice that it was determined to be a player in the quarter-mile wars. And lessons learned building these racers would translate into the company's high-performance street cars.

The 'Cuda Challenges the Big-Block Elite

It was 1969, the year Neil Armstrong left footprints on the moon, and for the 1969 model year, the Barracuda was undergoing more changes. It was also the year that the manufacturers had taken the gloves off. Chevrolet stuffed 427-ci race engines into street cars (L-88s and ZL-1s); Ford, in conjunction with Kar Kraft, was building Boss 429s in order to homolgate the engine for NASCAR competition.

Chrysler lagged behind. The 383 Magnum V-8 was the biggest engine offered for the production-based Barracuda. The insurance companies forced Washington to take notice of what these companies termed as the "inherently unsafe" musclecar. When Detroit got wind of the possibility that legislation could come down banning the hyper-performance market, it started to step away from developing high-performance cars. However, the pipeline was already full of high-performance products for the next couple of years. A pair of new Barracuda models were introduced at this time. Using the street slang term for the fish, the 'Cuda was born.

The 'Cuda 340 and 'Cuda 383 series were targeted toward the buyer that wanted to compete against the Mustangs, Camaros, and a host of pony cars. The carryover Formula S option was intended for the driver who enjoyed roads with turns. Equipped with a Hurst shifter and a heavy-duty suspension, the 'Cudas were able to blast down any curvy road. The 340 engine was unchanged, but the 383-ci engine was given a new camshaft, resulting in more power. The 383 provided 330 horsepower at 5,200 rpm, while the tire-melting torque of 410 foot-pounds came to a crescendo at 3,600 rpm. And as if this wasn't enough, in April 1969, Plymouth brought out its really big gun-the 440 'Cuda.

The 440 Magnum V-8 traces its roots back to the 383 family. Fitted with a set of free-breathing heads, the 440 produced buckets of power. Rated at 375 horsepower, it filled the relatively diminutive engine bay, so much so that power brakes, power steering, and air conditioning could not be wedged under the hood. Performance numbers illustrate that this big hammer of an engine was capable of producing big numbers. On the drag strip, it covered the quarter-mile at 104 miles per hour, and only needed 14.10 seconds to get there. This demonstrated that this package was capable of mixing it up with its competitors. With a massive engine over the front tires, the 440 'Cuda didn't negotiate corners with the same proficiency as a Boss 302 or Z/28. Of course, big-block aficionados didn't buy this car for its handling prowess, they bought it for its massive straight-line thrust. The only available transmission for use with the 440 was the TorqueFlite. One of two rear-axle ratios could be fitted, a 3.55:1 or 3.91:1. Either way, the driver needed to have the nose pointed in the desired direction before pressing the throttle.

The 1968 Barracuda 340 Formula S made curvy roads disappear in a hurry. In the January 1968 issue of *Motor Trend*, a similar vehicle covered the quarter-mile in 15.2 seconds at 92 miles per hour, yet the suspension was designed with road driving in mind. Good weight distribution was due to the lightweight 340-ci engine, which tipped the scales at 539 pounds dry. This excellent power plant was the standard mill in the 1968 Formula S package.

The Formula S option, on the other hand, was a scalpel able to rail through corners. The Formula S, housing the 340, was an especially well-rounded package. The fitting of power steering and power front disc brakes, heavy-duty one-inch shock absorbers, heavy-duty springs, torsion-bar front, and leaf rear provided the handling agility to keep up with its small-block competition. It helped the "driver who wants firm handling on all road surfaces. It puts more steel in the suspension, more restraint in the shock absorbers and more rubber on the road." The Formula S package could have either the Commando 340 or the Super Commando 383 V-8s. These were the same engines as used in the 'Cuda series.

But the end of the generation was at hand. A replacement for the A-body fish was initiated in 1967, and the time had come to replace the old warrior with a fresh look. The competition had rolled out new sheet metal, and the public was snapping it up by the hundreds of thousands. For model year 1969, only 31,987 Barracudas went to a good home, the lowest number since the first half-year sales in 1964. This was evidence enough for Chrysler to introduce an all-new model Barracuda. Excitement was to be spelled E-body.

The lineup for 1968 was identical to the prior year, when all three body styles were released. Chrysler was following the Ford Mustang in marketing a fastback, a coupe, and a convertible. The coupe was in production for three years, disappearing with the introduction of the E-body in 1970. With total sales in 1968 of 45,412 vehicles, this was to be the Barracuda's fourth most successful sales year. *Chrysler*

CHAPTER 3
E-BODY BREAKTHROUGH
BARRACUDA AND CHALLENGER 1970–1971

As the 1960s drew to a close, the high-performance car market reached its zenith. The market demand for ever higher power on the streets allowed Detroit to produce a score of tire-melting monsters. Chrysler was in the thick of it, with the Barracuda and Challenger leading the charge. The emphasis shifted from Gran Touring-type vehicles to straight-line, quarter-mile performance. Turning and stopping were not primary goals, instead the ability to pin the driver against the seatback at maximum thrust was the top priority. The E-bodies, especially when equipped with a big-block engine, took a back seat to no one. It was truly their finest hour.

E-Body Design and Development

The third-generation Barracuda was built on the new E-body platform, and work on the successor to the second-generation Barracuda started years before the release. Designer John Herlitz said, "Before the 1967 (model), Chrysler had spoken to Jaguar about a buyout in order to produce the new from the ground up car, but it was not in the cards from an investment standpoint."

Chrysler had gotten a look at the new Mercury Cougar, and noted that it was aimed at the "luxury GT" market. Also noted was the long-hood, short-rear-deck design that the Mustang had pioneered to good effect. The release of the Camaro/Firebird continued this trend, and both Ford and GM couldn't make enough of them. So the word at Chrysler was to build a viable entry in the hot pony car field. The basic shell was given to the respective stylists at Plymouth and Dodge. The Barracuda was intended to compete in the marketplace with the Mustang and Camaro/Firebird, while the Dodge was to be positioned against the Cougar, Chevelle, and the musclecars that embraced luxury. Both Mopars were offered in two body styles: coupe and convertible. While at first glance they

The fiberglass hood was identical to the 'Cuda AAR that competed in the 1970 Trans-Am racing series. The street and race cars also shared a common 340-ci block; however, the race car was destroked to 303.8 ci to comply with SCCA rules. Tiny winglets, fitted to the lower front corners, helped to extract downforce in the fledging years of race car aerodynamics.

The wide E-body engine compartment swallowed the ultra-wide Hemi engine with aplomb. This was not an accident. Chrysler required that the Barracuda/Challenger of 1970 be able to comfortably fit any and all engines in the Mopar roster. This 1971 Challenger R/T Hemi is a low-mileage survivor, and the large engine still leaves room for power steering and brakes.

With this argent hood scoop poking out from the Shaker Hood, the Hemi 'Cuda emblem instilled fear in any competitor. With massive black crackle valve covers, and the telltale trail of oil from the oil filler, the Hemi could intimidate anyone behind the wheel as well. Its factory rating of 425 horsepower was taken at 5,000 rpm, but that was a conservative rating and the engine was very happy at 6,000 rpm.

Power squared. The Panther Pink 1970 Hemi 'Cuda is one of just two built, while the 1971 Challenger R/T Hemi is a low-mileage original car. The long nose/short deck design, synonymous with the pony car, is evident in this view. The black "Hockey Stick" stripe, seen on the pink car, incorporated the engine size just in front of the rear edge. With a 426-ci engine under the hood, the word Hemi was written out.

looked similar, the only shared parts were the cowl structure, windshield, front torsion bars, and the rear leaf springs. The Barracuda had three models to pick from: the Barracuda, the luxury-oriented Gran Coupe and the gutsy 'Cuda. The Dodge aficionados were not ignored, with the fish's cousin coming in Challenger and Challenger Road/Track (R/T). These in turn came in a trio of flavors, hardtop, convertible, and Special Edition (SE). Dodge pitched the Challenger R/T in ads as "the pony with a

mean streak." Mean, nothing! This car could get vicious.

In the Plymouth studios, Herlitz was responsible for the outer skin of the third generation Barracuda. "This was a program that I worked very extensively on," Herlitz said. "I did the primary body design for the E-body, and I had a lot of help, such as Neil Walling on the front end. He did the grille and lamp setup." The hood was stretched, and the passenger compartment moved rearward one foot, and fitted a

The air cleaner assembly was visible through the hole in the hood, shaking and vibrating to the beat of the engine, hence the name "Shaker Hood." The top of the air cleaner could be ordered in one of three finishes: black, argent, or body color. The simulated vents on the front fenders were installed only on the 1971 model Plymouth E-bodies.

predecessor but its external dimensions changed. Overall length was reduced 6 inches, while width increased 5 inches, and the roofline was lowered 2 inches.

As Herlitz noted, "The whole idea on that car was to get a design that was very aggressive. We knew that Camaro and Mustang were out there with their own unique sheet metal, and this was our first shot at it. So what I tried to do was really spank the greenhouse [lower the roofline] on the car, particularly in the rear view. By carrying the tail lamps and that concavity across the rear, carrying it very high on the body, it made the roof in rear view appear like it was extremely low, particularly in the convertible version."

Designer Fred Schimmelphennig helped solve a design problem. "Because we had leaf spring rails coming straight through the stone pan (valence area beneath the rear bumper), he came up with the idea of the small, vertical bumperets," said Herlitz. "Using the bumperets and sweeping under the rest of the stone pan area in between those elements added all the grace in the world to the rear of the car."

Over in the Dodge Styling Studio, studio chief Bill Brownlie sketched what would eventually become the Challenger. He even came up with the name. The luxury emphasis compared to the Barracuda was evident in the use of brightwork and upgraded interior appointments. It rode on a longer wheelbase than the fish, 110 inches, and was longer by about 5 inches. Width grew by 1 1/3 inches and the Challenger ride height was 1 inch lower than the Barracuda's. The garage-filling width was necessary due to the corporate edict that the E-bodies would be able to use any engine in the Chrysler inventory, as well as installing any and all power accessories, including air conditioning. The front subframe and firewall from the B-body intermediates was the answer, allowing everything up to and including the Hemi to fit between the front wheels, with room to spare.

trunk so small, Plymouth would boast about it in its ads. Herlitz added that "You could get one set of golf clubs in there, if you had the Space-Saver spare. That was the requirement, one set of clubs." The rear quarter-panel line rose to meet the C-pillar, creating a hunched look, while the long, wide hood reminded some of a flight deck. At 108 inches, the wheelbase was identical to its

Moving the driver back exactly 12 inches allowed for the long hood/short deck look essential for the pony car stance. The 1970 'Cuda was Plymouth's answer to the Ford Mustang and General Motors Camaro and Firebird. The "In Violate" paint made a good color to contrast the white Hockey Stick tape graphics. High-back bucket seats were standard in the E-bodies but were a bit lacking in support.

The firewall was the starting point for the rest of the vehicle, locking in the "hard points," the location of the engine, suspension, and passenger placement. The firewall was one of the more expensive parts of any automobile to form, so significant cost savings would be realized if large parts could be lifted from other platforms. The B-body firewall gave Chrysler the option of installing seriously large engines under the broad hood. As Milt Antonick noted, "The E-body was a drag car," a sentiment echoed by John Herlitz: "In both the Hemi and 440 Six-Pak form, they were straight-line cars."

The interior was all new, too. Gone was the bright trim, replaced with acres of injected plastic. Faux wood on the dash and doors helped relieve the somber, austere cockpit. The high-back seats were a bit thin in the support department, but while behind the wheel, the driver faced a comprehensive and legible instrument cluster. The thin steering wheel was connected to a collapsible column. Gear shifting was dealt with by either a T-Shift connected to an automatic called the slap stick, or a Pistol-Grip four-speed shifter. Federally mandated side-door beams were fitted, starting in 1970, which made

The Challenger T/A option was available only in 1970 and was a street version of the Dodge Challenger Trans-Am race car driven by Sam Posey. This vehicle was painted SubLime, but the race car never had the T/A letters in the side stripes. Unlike the race car that had to use a single-four-barrel carburetor, the road version boasted of the trio of two-barrel carbs under the fiberglass hood.

the huge doors a bit unwieldy on a hill. Glass rattling in the door was the norm, but passengers tended to stay dry.

Plymouth and Dodge had a vast variety of paint color options to set their pony cars apart from the pack. The most vibrant were the "High-Impact" hues, which included paint code names like SubLime, Top Banana, TorRed, and Vitamin C. But these were just a few of the color codes available. A multitude of graphic tape packages gave the cars an aggressive look to match the car's inspiring performance.

Cubic-Inch War

In the quest to deliver brutal straight-line performance, Chrysler went the same path as the rest of Detroit–more cubic inches. While a vehicle equipped with a huge engine might not be able to turn or stop quickly, that was not the reason they existed. Getting from point A to B in a straight line as quickly as possible was reason enough to pour high-test into the tank. Fuel mileage was in the area of 6 miles per gallon with an aggressively driven Hemi.

When the E-bodies were introduced in model year 1970, buyers had an incredible array of engines to choose from. Nine power plants from the base 225-ci slant six that churned out 145 horsepower at 4,000 rpm to the brutal 425-horsepower 426-ci Hemi. In between was a diverse palette of power, including one 318, one version of a 340 mill, three models of the 383, and a pair of 440 big blocks.

The 225-ci slant six was the base engine in both the Challengers and Barracuda Gran Coupes. A floor-mounted shifter controlled a three-speed gearbox. The 318-ci engine was the entry-level V-8 power plant. From there, the two E-body models took divergent paths visually in the high-horsepower optional engines. It started out with a 335-horsepower 383-ci engine, topped with a single four-barrel carburetor. Optional engines included the 275-horsepower

On the prowl. This 1971 Hemi 'Cuda had little to fear in stoplight drag races. With the argent shaker air cleaner housing pulling in large amounts of atmosphere, the ground was guaranteed to blur by at an increasing rate. The bias-belted tires were of questionable worth in a turn, but they were the best street tires of the day.

Hemi: The Elephant in the Garage

The hemispherical-combustion-chamber cylinder head, or Hemi, was released to the public in 1951 as the Chrysler FirePower V-8. This engine displaced 331.1 ci and produced 180 horsepower at 4,000 rpm and 312 foot-pounds of torque at 2,000 rpm. The engine was head and shoulders above its competition, with its Hemi head design allowing superior breathing. With a near-centrally located spark plug and both intake and exhaust valve positioned for quick movement of gases, the engine was capable of impressive power.

But the cost, complexity, and weight of the Hemi pushed Chrysler to find a replacement, which was introduced in a passenger car in 1958. The Wedge-head design, the B-engine, replaced the first-generation Hemi as the 1958 model year drew to a close. But like a Phoenix, it would come back, to bask in glory.

Racing needs by Chrysler brought the Hemi design back into production. Circle-track racing required increasing amounts of vast power as well as durability. The Wedge engine was kicking butt in drag racing, but the NASCAR arena pushed Mopar to install a Hemi head on a raised-block 426-cid engine. The rush to get the engine ready for the season-opening 1964 Daytona 500 race was intense, but Chrysler engineers ended up with an incredible engine.

In order to continue racing the Hemi in NASCAR, Chrysler had to offer the engine to the public in street cars, so a detuned race engine was put on the option sheet. The compression was reduced to 10.25:1, and a milder cam was installed. Topped with twin Carter AFB carburetors, the power plant was listed as 425 horsepower at 5,000 rpm. However, the "Elephant," so nicknamed because of the huge valve covers, could live comfortably at 6,000 rpm, where the dyno registered close to 500 ponies. Just the thing to get a pony car down the road.

Rough-idling, noisy, thirsty, they were not the kind of engine one would put into a grocery-getter. They burned oil, changing the plugs was a real pain, and the cost of insuring a Hemi-equipped car could be frightening. The glint of a Hemi badge could be enough to discourage any knowledgeable competition. But when the revs came up, and you would side-step the clutch-well, hang on. You had better have it aimed right.

The last year of E-body Hemi production was 1971. The engine slipped into history for a number of reasons, including cost, complexity, and weight. But the final nail in the coffin was the difficulty in cleaning the monster engine up for the government-mandated clean air regulations. With only a minuscule number of Hemi engines fitted into 1971 E-bodies, it was not economically feasible to continue production. It was one of the finest racing engines ever designed, and though it is still popular on drag strips, it has been relegated to NASCAR history.

Topped by a pair of 550-cfm Carter AFB carburetors, the mechanically complex Hemi engine used long pushrods and long rocker arms to achieve the ideal hemispherical combustion chamber. The huge 2.25-inch intake valves allowed enough fuel/air mixture into the engine to generate 425 horsepower at 5,000 rpm.

Like the AAR 'Cudas that Dan Gurney and Swede Savage were strongarming around Trans-Am tracks, the production cars had the exhaust exit in front of the rear tires.

340, equipped with a four-barrel carb; two 440s, one four-barrel version rated at 375 horses, and the other at 390, courtesy of three two-barrel carburetors, otherwise known as the Six-Pak. The same setup was known as a "six barrel" in Plymouth cars. The 425-horsepower 426 Hemi, with its dual four-barrel carbs, resided at the top of the list.

The Challenger was offered with the same engine packages. A sport version called the R/T, short for Road/Track, was introduced in 1970. It featured a design component that was functional as well as head-turning-the "Shaker Hood." This option was only available on the 'Cuda models in the Plymouth camp and "sporty" Challengers with either a 440 Magnum V-8 or the 426 Hemi engine. The entire air cleaner assembly protruded from the center of the hood. This strong visual statement could be installed in one of three finishes: black, argent, or body color. The scoop quivered as the engine responded to acceleration. With the engine's displacement emblazoned on the sides of the scoop, it was a wonderful way to discourage pretenders from embarrassing themselves, especially if the two words "Hemi 'Cuda" reflected the glow from the streetlights.

Another luxury option for the Challenger was the aforementioned Special Edition, SE, which included a vinyl roof, a smaller rear window, an overhead interior console, leather-faced seats, and "SE" emblems scattered about. Engine choices were bewildering for the upscale E-body. The 340-ci engine was only available in the base model, putting out 275 horsepower, thanks to an unsilenced air cleaner and a functional hood scoop. The 335-horsepower 383 Magnum V-8 was the standard engine for the Challenger R/T. It also included heavy-duty drum brakes, Rallye suspension, a 3.23:1 axle ratio, and F70x14

fiberglass-belted tires, known for their comfortable ride when cold. When *Motor Trend* tested a Barracuda with this drivetrain in November 1969, the 'Cuda covered the quarter-mile in 14.9 seconds, with a trap speed of 91 miles per hour. Of course, options were the order of the day, and the engine bay could be filled to capacity. The $250 440-ci Magnum V-8 was fitted with either a single Carter four-barrel carburetor that produced 375 horsepower at 4,600 rpm or three Holley two-barrels, the Six-Pak option that generated 390 horsepower at 4,700 rpm. Filled with righteous internal parts like a shot-peened forged-steel crankshaft, heavy-duty connecting rods that had been Magnaglow inspected and aluminum pistons, the combustion chamber lived at 10.5:1 compression. The oil pump was the same unit used on the Hemi engine. But in the stoplight races these vehicles were intended to dominate, torque was king. And both 440s supplied that in prodigious amounts. With just under 500 foot-pounds of twist, the biggest problem was getting the tires to maintain any sort of grip with the ground. *Motor Trend* got its hands on a 'Cuda 440-6 for its May 1970 review, and the timing slip registered a run of 14.4 seconds at 100.0 miles per hour.

But for the buyer with deep pockets and a desire to visit the filling station frequently, the

The 1971 Hemi 'Cuda announced its arrival with vivid optional billboards declaring the size of the engine under the hood. The difficult-to-apply tape graphics were a one-year offering, little loved by the assembly line workers due to the occasional misalignment of body panels during vehicle assembly.

E-Bodies in Entertainment

Automobiles have been used by Hollywood since the early days of silent films. The action, drama, and presence of the "right" vehicle can turn a mediocre film into a memorable one. Who can forget the chase in *Bullit*, with a Mustang being chased around San Francisco by a Charger? And where would James Bond have been without his Aston Martin DB4?

So when the svelte E-body was rolled out in 1970, it wasn't long before it was on the silver screen. Theatergoers in 1971 could sit through 99 minutes of car-chasing color as a loner named Kowalski drove a white Dodge Challenger from Denver to ????? The film, *Vanishing Point*, was a wonderful escapist treat for gear-heads. The minutes the car was not on the screen could probably be counted on one hand, and it really captured the feel of the times, if not the driving styles.

Another occasion for an E-body sighting was everyone's favorite trio of crime-busters, *The Mod Squad*. From behind the wheel of a red 1971 convertible Challenger R/T, they fought their way to social justice in only 60 minutes. But I would like to know how their hair looked so good in a convertible.

Next stop, New York City, 1973, The Red Ball Garage, where *Car & Driver* editor Brock Yates sits behind the wheel of a white 1973 Dodge Challenger.

Having a hard time telling these 1971 Hemi 'Cuda convertibles apart? So does the crew of the TV show *Nash Bridges*. In fact, none of the vehicles are Hemis. Three of the cars are equipped instead with 440-ci engines and automatic transmissions, while the fourth has a 360 mill and a four-speed. *Robert Genat/Zone Five Photo*

(What is it about white Challengers?) It's the second running of the Cannonball Sea-To-Shining Sea Memorial Trophy Dash, a flat-out run across the United States, ending at the Portofino restaurant in Redondo Beach, California. Due to weather, navigational mix-ups and, well... stuff, the Dodge has to settle for second place, missing the checkered by only 10 minutes. Thirty-seven hours, 26 minutes is a long time in a Challenger, especially with two other guys. The race inspired Hollywood to make a movie, *Cannonball Run*, with Burt Reynolds. Entertainment comes in all grades.

Recently, the E-body has been on the screen again, albeit the small one. Don Johnson, formerly known as the Ferrari-driving detective on *Miami Vice*, now plays a Plymouth-driving detective in *Nash Bridges*. Set in San Francisco, the good guy chases the perps in a yellow 1971 Hemi 'Cuda Convertible. Except that's no Hemi. In fact, four cars are used in the series, one a 360-cid engine four-speed and the rest with 440s. Curious Yellow was the desired color, but it was found that a car painted that shade just didn't look right on film. Repainting the vehicles a Sherwin Williams industrial color, "school bus yellow" got the look on film that the producers wanted. So what you see isn't real, like most of Hollywood. But it is entertaining.

This 1971 Challenger R/T convertible was eye candy on the early 1970s cop show *The Mod Squad*. The side tape graphic that ended above the beltline kick-up was unique to the 1971 Dodge E-body.

The wide 440-ci engine did not leave a lot of spare room in the engine bay of a 'Cuda. Note the tight fit between the right-side exhaust manifold and the shock tower. This power plant was much easier to live with, on a day-to-day basis, than the famed Hemi. With 390 horsepower, the three-carb Six-Pak option did not lack for motivation.

Hemi was the ultimate big-block weapon for the street. Covered in depth elsewhere in this book, the Hemi was a justifiable legend in its own time. Built with pure racing in mind, it lived to rev. Herlitz said, "I had a company car, a triple-black Hemi 'Cuda convertible, and I used to face off against a friend of mine who had a 440 Six-Pak convertible. We used to scream up Oakland Avenue with those cars. He would pull me at about a car length up to about 60 miles per hour. Then at 60, I would pass him like he was standing still." While not cheap, this $1,227.50 option ensured that the driver was always paying attention to actually driving. When this monster

was slipped under the hood, the drivetrain came with a Dana 60, 8 3/4-inch axle if the manual transmission was ordered. The 727 TorqueFlite absorbed the shock of full power shifts. The gear-set was offered as a Trak Pak, which meant a 3.54:1 Sure-Grip limited slip differential, or the Super Trak Pak, the same thing except for the 4.10:1 gears.

In the June 1970 issue of *Road Test*, a Dodge Hemi Challenger fitted with a four-speed and 4.10:1 gears flew down the drag strip in 14 seconds flat, tripping the lights at 104 miles per hour. *Motor Trend* pulled similar numbers in the May 1970 magazine; 14.0 sec-

With a gang of six barrels to direct the fuel/air mixture, the exceptional 340-ci engine delivered a consistently rated 290 horsepower in the 1970 AAR 'Cuda. A NACA-type hood scoop fed the 10.5:1 compression engine plenty of fresh air.

onds at 102.0 miles per hour. Sixty miles per hour would come up on the speedometer in only 5.8 seconds. And this was on street tires of the era! Motion was needed to stay cool: Air conditioning was not available with the Hemi. This engine was basically the street version of a racing engine, with all the pros and cons. It cast a very big halo over the entire E-body line. Chrysler was wise to put the E-bodies on the market with the high-performance goodies available from day one. The company had learned from the Valiant Barracuda days, when the vehicle was a repackaged economy car. This time, it was full bore, right out of the box.

Trans-Am Racer Replicas

Chrysler was a bit tardy in getting a factory entry into the SCCA's Trans-Am racing series. Both Ford and General Motors had been slugging it out with Boss 302s and Camaro Z-28s. The gang at Mopar wanted some racing glory to rub off onto the line of street cars, so they dove into the fray for the 1970 racing season. The rules required that the manufacturer build 2,500 street models of its racing car. To this end, Chrysler released the All-American Racers (AAR) 'Cuda and its cousin, the T/A Challenger. Production was just enough to meet the rules, with 2,724 AARs built, while 2,142 Challenger

With the smallest displacement "B" engine big block, the 1970 Challenger R/T was a formidable package. The 383-ci mill breathed through a single four-barrel carburetor, releasing 330 horsepower at opportune moments. Trim rings highlighted the 15-inch wheels.

T/As were put on the road. All of these vehicles were built in a five-week period in March and April of 1970. Regardless which corporate division made the vehicle, both models were superb road machines. A black-matte fiberglass hood, complete with a NACA-style air scoop, separated the AAR 'Cuda from the other production cars. This hood was designed by Milt Antonick on location at "Creative Engineering," a Detroit job shop. The scoop originally incorporated a center split, but was removed from the production hood due to insufficient airflow. A graphic tape, made by 3M, was used to good effect, creating a strobelike side stripe. Studio engineer

Clint Washburn designed the strobe effect in a few hours, calculating a four percent change in each line's thickness to achieve the desired pattern. Unlike the racers, which had to use a 340-ci engine destroked to 303.8 ci and topped with a single four-barrel carburetor, the street versions were powered by a Six-Pak-equipped 340-ci engine.

This proven power plant was unique to the T/A and AAR. The iron block was stress relieved, and the main bearing area, while delivered with two-bolt main bearings, had plenty of material for the fitting of four-bolt main bearing caps. The rest of the engine had attention lavished on it, including the triple two-barrel carburetor setup

Designed to facilitate rapid gear changes in competition, the Hurst Pistol Grip enjoyed the Hurst reputation for bulletproof reliability. It required a firm hand, but once it dropped into a gear, there was no mistaking that feeling of a well-crafted component.

The Slap-Stik, controlling the durable TorqueFlite automatic transmission, helped lower ETs by allowing a single-gear upshift simply by slapping the shifter handle forward. This came in handy when a driver was simply trying to keep a large-engined E-body pointed in the correct direction.

Chrysler ads boasted that the E-body had the smallest trunk in its class. With about six cubic feet, the space-saver spare was appreciated. It was difficult to smuggle many people into a drive-in with these vehicles.

on the aluminum intake manifold. The engine was rated at 290 horsepower at 5,000 rpm, but redline came up at 6,500. Turns could be taken with more confidence than in a big block, which had a tendency to push into an aggressively taken corner. The lighter weight over the front E60x15 tires meant that the power could be applied sooner and more spiritedly to the G60x15 rear tires. Helping to slow all that kinetic energy down was the front disc/rear drum package, standard for the AAR-T/A. Inside the rear axle was a set of 3.55:1 gears, which helped this package deliver a dash from a stop to 60 miles per hour in 5.8 seconds for *Car & Driver* magazine in its July 1970 issue.

The editors took an AAR down the quarter-mile in 14.3 seconds, covering the finish line at 99 miles per hour. *Car & Driver* noted that quality control was still something of a struggle, but when the bugs were worked out, it promised to be a formidable package.

The Challenger T/A was modeled after the Trans-Am racer that Sam Posey wheeled around the Trans-Am series. Its fiberglass hood was influenced by the belly air scoop on the P-51 Mustang fighter plane, and Dodge pulled it off beautifully. The raised inlet allowed the engine to ingest fresh, cool air,

continued on page 66

A pair of big-block 1971 'Cudas in their element. Waiting for the lights to descend is a 440-ci-equipped convertible and a Hemi 'Cuda coupe. Off the line, the 440 gets the jump, but as the engines wind out, the high-revving Hemi would come into its own. Either vehicle promised a memorable ride. *Robert Genat/Zone Five Photo*

A 1971 Hemi 'Cuda rolls out into the night in search of prey. Until they were warm, the Polyglas GT tires felt anything but round. The radio was useful as a dashboard decoration: the Hemi engine tended to drown out whatever the radio was playing.

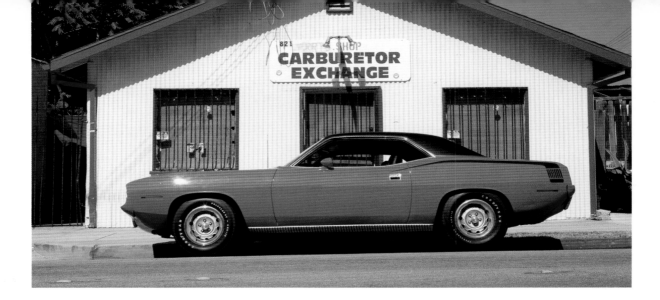

A pair of 550-cfm Carter AFBs sit on top of the 426-ci Hemi engine. The optional vinyl top contrasted well with the Panther Pink paint. This is one of two such cars believed to be in existence.

When a buyer went to a dealership to purchase a 1970 Challenger R/T, one of the decisions to be made was whether to equip the car with a longitudinal tape stripe of a bumblebee tape appliqué at the rear. The dual exhaust helped the engine to breathe as well as produce a rich bass note.

The 1970 Dodge Challenger T/A 340 Six-Pak was one of the finest driving pony cars to come out of the heyday of Detroit muscle. The huge hood scoop was functional, and after a few minutes behind the wheel, the driver would not even notice it. Disc brakes were standard (and appreciated).

In-Violet was the name of the color, and it appealed to the youth market the 1970 'Cuda was intended for. With the engine displacement where all the world could see, it was easy to match vehicle performance with like-minded drivers on a warm Saturday night. Quick to rev, the 340-ci engine could acquit itself very well.

continued from page 61

not the stagnant boundary layer of air clinging to the hood surface. A side stripe and graphic behind the front wheels proclaimed its racing lineage, as well as the megaphone exhaust tips in front of the rear tires. The street versions of Chrysler's race cars were the only E-bodies that put the radio antenna on the rear fender, due to the use of the fiberglass hood. Reception with the glass hood was less than ideal.

An Upgraded Suspension

What good is power if it can't be put down? Chrysler hit up the parts bin when putting the suspension together. The front torsion bars, a Barracuda staple since 1964, were carried over on the E-body. The front subframe, big enough to cradle any large engine in the Chrysler inventory, was taken from the B-body intermediates, as was the rear suspension. A wide rear track of

The 440-powered 1970 'Cuda was a formidable street fighter. The bulges behind the rear bumper guards hid the rear leaf spring purchases. The flow-through exhaust was little loved by the assembly line: tighter build alignment was required.

60.7 inches allowed the use of the wide tires, necessary for traction and sales. A fat .94-inch antiroll bar was bolted to the rear with some engine combinations. The semi-elliptical leaf springs, attached to the live rear axle, had the difficult job of maintaining contact between rolling stock and road. When a big-block engine found its way under the hood, the rear springs had varying amounts and lengths of leafs. Typically, the big-block engines possessed more leaf springs to handle the enormous torque.

While the emphasis in these years was ultimate speed, brake performance was important, if not vital. Drum brakes were standard, and front disc brakes were an option, except for the AAR-T/A 340 Six Pak. These automobiles came with 11-inch power front disc brakes with semi-metallic linings and 11-inch rear drums. This was an effective package, an AAR coming to a stop from 80 miles per hour in 220 feet according to a July 1970 *Car & Driver* test.

Second-Year E-Body Cars

Sales for the E-body in model year 1970 were not the stuff of accountants' dreams. The Barracuda boasted its third-best sales year ever with 55,499 fish swimming out of dealerships, while 83,032 Challengers rolled into the public's hands. Chrysler was getting strong signals that the muscle pony car market was starting to go

The deep-set grille was home to the combination parking lights/turn signals. The Go-Wing on the trunk was manually adjusted for downforce. The Deep Burnt Orange Metallic was not a common color, and the power-operated convertible top let the sunset fill the copper interior.

The 1971 Hemi 'Cuda's narrow tires were laughably inadequate to translate the massive torque into miles per hour. The graceful bumpers were little more than chrome accents to the overall body design.

soft, just as it jumped into the pool. The insurance on the big-block models could run to 100 percent of the monthly vehicle payment and the safety zealots were marching to Washington, D.C., to protest the availability of healthy automobiles to the public. It was in this confused market that Plymouth and Dodge rolled the E-bodies into their second year.

The sophomore year of E-body manufacturing saw little engineering change to the Barracuda and Challenger. Minor revisions to the grille and rear, except that the entire Barracuda line now lit the way with four headlights, just like the Challenger. An attractive set of four nonfunctional gills were set in the front fenders of the Barracuda, and the grille could be had in

With four headlights, this Hemi 'Cuda must be a 1971 model. The other quick giveaways are the louvers on the front fenders, also a solo-year stylistic addition. With a sight like this in the rearview mirrors, moving aside would be a prudent move. The only indication of the power plant is the script on the cold-air Shaker Hood, a subtle way to trounce pretenders.

either argent or body color. A set of simulated scoops in front of the rear wheels were optional on the Challenger. The underhood offerings were carried over from 1970, with the exception of the 440 engine equipped with a single four-barrel carburetor and the bottom-tier 383, which were dropped. The Challenger R/T convertible was also cut from the lineup, as only 1,070 were sold in 1970, leaving ragtop performance to the 'Cuda. The AAR 'Cuda and Challenger T/A were discontinued as well, due to the pulling of Mopars from the SCCA's Trans-Am series at the end of the 1970 racing season.

Interior upgrades were minimal, consisting of seat cushion changes and fabrics. The normal profusion of options awaited the buyer, allowing the company to tailor the vehicle to individual tastes. Power windows, leather, even a tape recorder to help remember those special motoring moments. Graphic packages grew even more outlandish, the 'Cuda wearing optional "billboards," announcing to one and all the cubic-inch displacement of the engine. Subtlety was not part of the vocabulary.

High-Performance Decline

The bean counters were not happy. Sales in

With the top of the air filter assembly peering through the Shaker Hood opening, this 1970 440 Six-Pak could be looking for worthy rivals.

1971 were dismal. As the new kid on the block, great things were expected from the Challenger. But when sales plummeted to 29,883, a hard look at the pony car market was in order. The Barracuda posted even more subterranean sales numbers. Total fish sold in 1971 was only 18,690, a frighteningly low number. Hemis were not exactly selling like gangbusters, as the musclecar era was winding to a close. With only 115 of the 426-ci monsters occupying a 1971 'Cuda, and fewer than 75 Challenger Hemi R/Ts built,

the stage was set for the demise of performance. The arrival of emission controls and low-lead gasoline spelled the end of the line for the street Hemi. It was too expensive for Mopar to clean the beast up for street use, thus it was shown the door. Unfortunately, it stepped off the stage in 1972, accompanied by most of the performance engines in the stable. Plymouth and Dodge had introduced their entries into the muscle pony car ranks two years too late. It would doom the cars to history.

CHAPTER 4

THE MEEK SHALL INHERIT . . .

BARRACUDA AND CHALLENGER 1972–1974

Hyper-performance pony cars had seen slipping sales since 1970, and insurance rates for the musclecars were climbing like a Saturn V rocket. Gone were vehicles that shook the garage upon ignition; only a handful were left, like the Firebird Trans Am SD-455 and the Chevelle SS. The introduction of low-lead fuel and government-mandated safety equipment meant that the enemy of velocity was at hand: lowered compression ratios and additional weight. Worse, the public was expressing an interest in smaller, more fuel-efficient cars. *Motor Trend* magazine actually crowned the Chevrolet Vega its Car of the Year for 1971. The pendulum was swinging away from automobiles that could swallow quarter-mile-long stretches of road in a single gulp to transport that was more environmentally friendly, safety-minded, and mileage-conscious. With the technology of the day, that meant exorcising excitement from the E-body. The Chrysler pony cars were like the dinosaurs moments after the asteroid struck, doomed to extinction, just not there yet.

Changing Times and the Changed E-Bodies

The changes wrought on the E-bodies for the 1972 were profound. Visually, nothing significant. The shaker hoods were gone, the grilles were massaged, and the taillights altered. No profound styling change took place, just the yearly Detroit freshening. The more wild styling tricks such as side exhaust, tape graphics, and hood pins were absent, replaced with the standard color offerings, simple stripes down the sides and tame, nonfunctional hood scoops. The fish was available in only two flavors, both in coupe form: the Barracuda and the 'Cuda. After one year using four headlamps to show the way, the crew at Plymouth rolled their pony car out with two headlights again. The Challenger was no better off, with the only choices being the standard

The 1974 E-bodies were the swan song for the Chrysler pony cars. This example was the last 'Cuda ever to roll down the assembly line. It was one of the 17 built in Avocado Green. It was equipped with a 360-ci engine and a manual four-speed; the Power Bulges on the hood hinted at former glory.

The round taillights are a quick means of identifying a post-performance Barracuda or 'Cuda. The heavy-duty bumper pads were a low-cost fix, allowing Chrysler to meet new government bumper regulations. The tape stripe was rather tame compared to prior years.

hardtop coupe and the Rallye, which replaced the R/T. Nonfunctional louvers behind the front wheels were highlighted with a tape graphic on the Challenger Rallye. The Dodge E-body sported a different grille and rear treatment. The "sad mouth" front grille was a questionable styling change, but when one looks at what happened to the rest of the car, the grille was the least of its problems. The Challenger brochure for 1972 sort of put the past into perspective: "The way things are today, maybe what you need is not the world's hottest car." It was plainly evident that performance was on a steep decline.

The interior of Chrysler's pony cars had a bit of attention given them, primarily in the form of improved seats. The Rallye Instrument Cluster was standard on the Rallye model Challenger and an option in the base model. The Plymouth version had the same changes on the inside, with the Barracuda and 'Cuda mirroring the Dodge. That was it in the cockpit.

Sweeping changes were the order of the day under the hood. All of the big blocks were swept out, reducing engine options to three. The long-toothed slant six, all 225 ci, was the standard engine in the Barracuda and Challenger. This bulletproof mill cranked out 110 reliable horsepower. Stepping up one notch in the food chain put you near the top. Both the Challenger Rallye and the 'Cuda had the 318-ci, two-barrel V-8

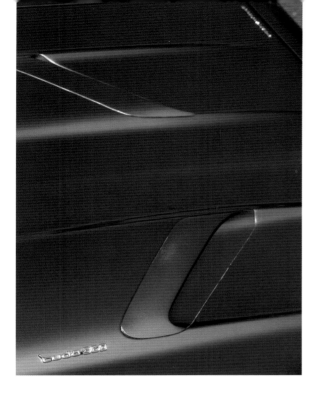

The blistered hood on a 1974 'Cuda meant that a 360-ci engine was underneath. If a 1974 Barracuda sported a smooth hood, then the vehicle had a 318-ci engine installed. Hood pins and wild graphics were a thing of the past.

The 360-ci engine was lifted from the large passenger vehicles in the Chrysler catalog. This power plant replaced the 340 engine due to the 360 being easier to certify for emission regulations. Rated at 245 horsepower, the engine could drag a 'Cuda up to 116 miles per hour.

engine under the hood. With the engine's 150 net horsepower, few would be fooled into thinking they could pull down a Hemi. Starting in the 1972 model year, engine output was not expressed in brake horsepower. Cars were rated in a "real-world" fashion with accessories bolted on and working, along with an often-restrictive exhaust system. This SAE net horsepower rating was far more realistic in regard to what was turning the rear wheels, but the torque and horsepower figures paled in comparison to the old system. The optional engine in the Barracuda and Challenger was standard in the 'Cuda and Challenger Rallye. That was the 340-ci engine, complete with a four-barrel carburetor. It produced 240 horses, not quite in the same arena as the prior couple of years. But that was the pony car market: turning its back on the very vehicles

that were lusted after only a few short years before. As the Challenger ads put it: "Maybe what you need is a well-balanced, thoroughly instrumented road machine." Indeed.

Weathering the Storm

Sales for the 1972 model year were steady, with 18,450 Plymouth pony cars sold, while the Dodge Boys unloaded 26,663. The pony cars had never been a high-volume platform for Chrysler, instead drawing potential buyers into the showrooms, where they would sign on the dotted line for a Valiant or Duster. The Barracuda faced competition from its stablemate, the Duster 340. Lighter than a Barracuda by 285 pounds, it was quicker in the quarter-mile by almost one full second. And it cost less, a critical factor to the 18- to 30-year-old target

Round taillights were introduced on the Barracuda and 'Cuda in 1972. Plymouth's answer to bumper regulations was to install larger pads, an understandable action with the end of production coming on April 1, 1974, producing total Barracuda model-year numbers of only 11,734 vehicles.

market. Chrysler was treating the E-bodies like an unwanted stepchild, born in an era of cheap gas and few regulations. The Big Three were scrambling for entries in the compact field, so the Barracuda/Challenger were left to fend for themselves.

When the 1973 line was unveiled, performance slid further down the slippery slope, and engine options were simplified and streamlined. The slant six engine was no longer offered in an E-body. The only power plants available were the 318- and 340-ci engines, the latter the standard mill in the 'Cuda. These were not changed from the prior year, so neck-snapping acceleration of yore was missing. However, *World Cars* tested a

pair of Barracudas: The vehicle equipped with the 318-ci engine delivered a top speed of 104 miles per hour, while the 340-ci engine rocketed up to 115 miles per hour.

The Challenger ads used the tag line "Quiet Good Taste," and that was valid, but the writing was on the wall. Along with the Barracuda, the Dodge had minimal changes on the exterior, primarily 5-mile-per-hour bumper pads on the front bumper, courtesy of the government. The Challenger Rallye was now no longer a separate model but an option package, and with the top-of-the-line 340-ci engine churning away, a TorqueFlite-equipped vehicle ran the

Dodge followed the same course at Plymouth in the bumper department. This 1974 Challenger is one of the last 15 built, and the 360-ci engine and four-speed transmission still dish out plenty of fun, if not the neck-snapping acceleration of a 440 or a Hemi.

The "sad mouth" grille made its debut on the 1972 Challenger, and was retained for the rest of the production run. This 1974 Challenger hid a 360 under the simulated air inlets on the hood.

quarter-mile in 16.3 seconds, flashing across the line at 85 miles per hour, a respectable time for that year of production. It was pathetic, however, compared to numbers produced in 1970, and it was a shadow of its former self.

But the cars were selling, just not in the volume that would bring warmth to a bean counter's heart. Chrysler sold 32,596 Challengers and 22,213 Barracudas during the 1973 model year. This was an improvement from the year before, but not a big enough rise to prevent the inevitable. Body changes were nil, while underhood improvements were minimal. Electronic ignition was introduced, as were hardened valve seats in the cylinder heads for use with unleaded gasoline. The seats were modified for improved comfort. The option list was still a mile long, but power windows, remote control mirrors, and an 8-track player do not a muscle-car make.

Simulated vents located on the front quarter panels used a strobe tape graphic to denote performance, quite a change from the days when the tires would leave similar marks on the road.

Curtain Call for the Legend

The 1974 model year looked a bit better as the new E-bodies were released-at least on paper. The rest of the pony car industry was in the tank. Even Ford's Mustang was responding to market forces, introducing the new Mustang II, which *Motor Trend* magazine declared its Car of the Year for 1974. It would rack up 385,993 units sold that year. The future of the Mopar pony car and all other pony cars was in doubt.

The Arab oil embargo put the final nail in the pony car coffin and dramatically changed the American automotive market. Long lines at the gas stations and even/odd fill-up days did not put a pleasant taste in the mouth of the American motorist. Small, fuel-sipping engines were now the desired form of propulsion. This was the perfect time for Chrysler to shuffle its power plants. The 340-ci engine was no longer in the lineup, replaced with an even bigger

The Carter Thermo-Quad four-barrel carburetor was the fuel-mixer on the 340-ci engine as fitted in the 1973 Challenger Rallye. The Rallye option included this 240 horsepower mill, but the upper portion of the 150-mile-per-hour speedometer was safe from being worn out.

The 1974 'Cuda showed the effects of Washington, D.C., telling Detroit to improve the bumpers' ability to protect the vehicle body. This 360, four-speed E-body was the last 'Cuda to be built. It's code KJ6, Avocado Gold Metallic—a color of the times if ever there was one.

Behind the Wheel of a T/A 340

Who says you can never go home? Growing up in the Midwest, I was in high school when the really cool cars hit the street. The guys driving the big-engined E-bodies were looked at like rebels. We thought that Chevelles and Mustangs were the way to go. Then some slippery 'Cuda or Challenger would slither past, menace in its wake. The day came when I got a ride with a bored owner, wanting to see the look of terror on my face when he planted the pedal.

Now I was behind the wheel, almost 30 years later. In front of me sat a 1970 Challenger T/A, 340 Six-Pak, connected to the rear tires by a Hurst shifter that fit my hand like the control stick in an F-4 Phantom II. I twisted the key, hearing the distinctive Chrysler starter spin the engine. A poke at the accelerator, and the engine barked its greeting. The trumpet side-exhaust pipe was an arm's reach from my ears, and it sounded like Mr. Peabody's Way Back Machine. I reached to close the door and pulled the long span of metal and plastic toward me. After a while, the door glass stopped rattling, and I wiggled on the flat seat, trying to get a little bit more legroom, but to no avail. The large, thin-rimmed steering wheel was inches from my chest, like a NASCAR racer, or a pre-war Bugatti. The lo-o-o-ong clutch pedal gave me no clue of an engagement point, so I firmly gripped the shifter and pushed the meaty lever into reverse. I let out the left pedal slowly, finally it caught. Spin the wheel, what fun! The steering wheel felt exactly like an early video game in an arcade. Absolutely zero feel, but what the screen was showing seemed related to what I was doing. This Challenger T/A was the same, only the view over the huge hood scoop was not as good as the video game.

But there was no mistaking the purpose of the noisemaker under that expanse of fiberglass. It felt that it could and would willingly rev to the point where connecting rods started coming through cast iron. When the tachometer reached 3,000, the pair of carburetors flanking the primary center two-barrel opened, delivering the most wonderful rush of power I had felt in years. The Hurst shifter fell readily to hand, and while it took a firm effort to catch the next gear cleanly, it was never excessive. The engine/transmission

Poised for takeoff, this 1970 Challenger T/A 340 Six-Pak provided this author with no small amount of pleasure. The radio antenna was mounted on the rear fender of both this model and the AAR 'Cuda because the fiberglass hoods interfered with radio reception.

The thin-rimmed steering wheel was too close to the chest and provided zero room, but the Pistol-Grip shifter fell easily into the hand. With the 340-ci engine under the flat black hood, the 1970 Challenger T/A was a superb road machine.

combo worked beautifully together, perfectly matched for the job at hand. Yet the vehicle never let me forget that what I was handling was a machine. The brakes, disc/drum worked evenly and gave acceptable slowing, at least while they were cool. I wasn't going to get them hot to the point of fade.

The handling was pure vintage early 1970s, which is a polite way of saying a firm ride, moderate body roll, and tiptoeing through the corners. Sometimes age can be on my side, as memory told me that the wheels had better be arrow straight before I got enthusiastic about the accelerator. The tach needle raced around the small face, but I was shifting by ear and memory. In fourth gear, three grand, 65 miles per hour. A gentle push on the pedal, and the engine spun faster, right now! No pause, no stumble, just pure, seamless thrust. Purely addictive.

Time to put the toy away, and I thought it was much too early. But I didn't own it, so I headed toward the barn. But the final stop sign brought me to a halt. I pushed the engine up to 4,000, sidestepped the clutch, heard the bellow of mechanical joy, and felt the rear tires scrabble and claw for traction. The rear end was gently swaying from side to side as I stayed on the power and made slight steering corrections. Finally, the rubber gained purchase, and the seatback felt for my vertebrae. Backing off the gas just a bit, I grabbed second gear, then hard on the accelerator as I brought the clutch pedal up as fast as I could. The back end squatted for a second, the tires barked their pleasure, and I was at the next corner. Damn. I rolled into the driveway, reached around the wheel and shut it down. I could feel the smile stuck on my face. Who said you can never go home?

The grille of the 1974 'Cuda was the only one that was trimmed in red. The simulated hood scoops look like gills laid on their side, and they were a good place to mount the engine displacement logo, in this case a 360 four-barrel engine.

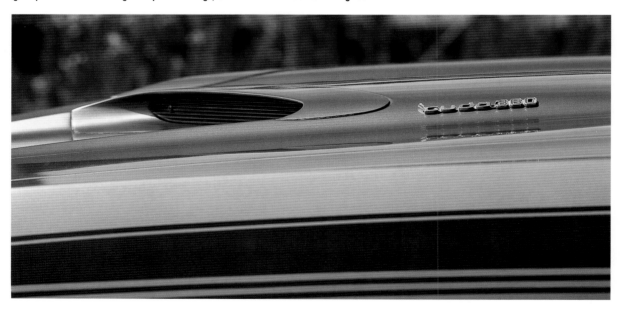

The Last Hurrah. Introduced for the 1974 model year, the 360 passenger car engine replaced the famed 340 mill. This engine was a shadow of the fire-breathers of yore, but actually did a good job, when one considers the sophistication (or lack) of the emission controls of the day.

Don Hood designed this full-scale mock-up. It demonstrated the design direction Chrysler was pursuing with the proposed new F-body car, the successor of the E-body. The clay over wood form was built on an armature, a frame constructed of 6x6-inch L-section aluminum strips. This photograph is dated April 14, 1969. *Milt Antonick collection*

engine, the new 360-ci V-8, rated at 245 horse-power. This engine was standard on the 'Cuda and could be installed on the Barracuda for only $259. At 245 horsepower, performance was just appalling. This engine was brought onto the scene due to its being easier to certify for emission regulations.

The only visible change for 1974 was the addition of rear bumpers that would handle the government-mandated collision standards-just what the E-bodies needed, more weight. But the debate was reduced to a moot point, when on April 1, 1974, Chrysler shut down the production lines for the Barracuda and Challenger, 10 years to the day from the start of Barracuda production. The car that started life as a fastback Valiant had grown into one of the all-time great musclecars during 1969-1970, but its performance demise was slow and agonizing from 1971 to 1974. The once-proud model was a shell of its former self, and it was time for Chrysler to draw the curtain. Only 6,745 Barracudas and 4,989 'Cudas were built for model year 1974. The Dodge camp was not exactly popping the champagne, as only 16,437 Challengers were put together before the

plug was pulled. As Herlitz stated, "What we tried to do was hang on to the success of the Roadrunner: it went from a volume standpoint that just roared right past the Barracuda and Challenger in sales."

The bubbly was flowing in Chevrolet/Pontiac offices. The Camaro and the Firebird were the only true pony cars left, and over the years sales would rebound for the pair. They had the market to themselves, and until the Mustang returned to its roots in 1979, these cars were the only show in town. A successor to the E-body was under way in the Chrysler design studios as far back as 1969, but the evaporating pony car market killed the vehicle before it ever turned a wheel. The stillborn "F-body" would have been a reskin of the E-body, utilizing the firewall and windshield of the B-body intermediates. Chrysler seemed to put one wrong foot in front of another in the 1970s. *Car & Driver* magazine put it into perspective: "Chrysler doesn't do anything first. Instead, it carefully watches what everybody else in Detroit is doing and when it sees an area of abnormal market activity it leaps onto that spot. Because it always leaps late-which is inevitable if it doesn't begin to prepare its entry into the market until someone else already has one-it tries to make up for being late by jumping into said spot harder than everyone else." This might be the epitaph for the Barracuda and Challenger. The Chrysler Corporation of today is a different world, a true leader. What would a car like the E-bodies be like today?

This shows a proposed frontal view of the F-body. A mirror placed on the design study's centerline, allowing a balanced look of essentially two designs on one clay mock-up. *Milt Antonick collection*

CHAPTER 5

RACING INTO THE RECORD BOOKS

BARRACUDA AND CHALLENGER COMPETITION CARS

Since the earliest days of the automobile, pitting one vehicle against others has been a source of pleasure and pain. The Barracuda was no exception. Competing in race venues such as the drag strip and road courses, as well as the stoplight, has proven that the Barracuda, and later the Challenger, could hold its own against the best that other Detroit manufacturers could field. Even today, the Chrysler pony car is popular with competitors and crowds alike.

Not long after the Barracuda was released, drag strips saw the Plymouth at the start line. The Commando 273-ci engine responded well to high-performance modification. During the 1965 season, the Golden Commandos' Goldfish, out of Detroit, competed with a steel-bodied Barracuda. It fought in the F/Stock class, and won the class championship at the 1965 NHRA Nationals with a run of 13.47 seconds, crossing the line at 103.68 miles per hour. Another 1965 Barracuda was guided down the quarter-mile by famed stock-car champion Richard Petty. The folks at NASCAR had ruled that the

Hemi race engine, so dominant in the 1964 NASCAR season, would be outlawed. Its power advantage over the Ford entries helped Petty to walk away with the title. To eliminate the "unfair advantage," the Hemi was shut out. Chrysler responded by starting out the season sitting out stock car racing. Instead, Petty got a 1965 Barracuda and a Hemi engine, painted it Petty's famous blue, and started pulling speeds in excess of 140 miles per hour in 10 seconds down the quarter-mile. Called "Outlawed," it was equipped with dual carburetors and a TorqueFlite automatic transmission. Later in the season, the label "43/JR" appeared on the side,

The 1970 Challenger Trans-Am race car, driven in the 1970 season by Sam Posey, is seen being threaded through the famed Corkscrew at Laguna Seca during the 1999 Monterey Historic Races. Posey was less than thrilled with the SubLime paint, and covered as much of the vivid color as possible with black paint. At the 1970 season-opening race here, Posey glanced down to see the track flashing underneath the car, as the acid-dipped unibody had developed cracks in the tunnel and floor.

The Keith Black-prepared engine was actually a destroked 340 block, displacing 303.8 ci, so it complied to the 305-ci rule. Breathing through a single Holley four-barrel carburetor, the heavily massaged mill would crank out 460 horsepower all day. Note the aluminum Harrison coolant expansion tank lifted from a midyear Corvette Sting Ray.

The office of the Posey Trans-Am Challenger was basic race car—that is, Spartan. The racing bucket held the driver firmly behind the steering wheel in turns, and the roll cage protected the driver in a crash as well as bracing the body-connecting the front and rear subframes. Posey was surprised at how wide the vehicle seemed from inside, feeling that he could block the whole track with a jab of the accelerator.

and Hilburn fuel injection, a Chrysler four-speed transmission, and a fiberglass front end were added to help the drag car find the finish line in a brisk fashion. Petty ran the Barracuda until late July 1965, when NASCAR rescinded the Hemi ruling and allowed the "Elephant" engine back on its tracks. Petty went back to making left turns.

Probably the most famous Barracuda to compete a quarter-mile at a time was the Hemi Under Glass. Constructed by Jack Watson at the Hurst Research Center in Michigan, it was "A Rolling Research Laboratory." This vehicle had a 426 Hemi engine, located behind the driver in the space that the rear seat and luggage area usually took up. At first fitted with a manual transmission and a Hurst shifter, it used an independent rear suspension. A few passes later, the hand-crafted rear was replaced with a solid rear axle. The driver twisted his head a bit sideways to see the line down the side of the strip. Later, a 14 x16 inch Plexiglas window was installed next to the gas pedal, allowing a better view of the track. Famous for holding a wheelstand the entire length of the drag strip, the vehicle's first full-throttle run on 65 percent nitro resulted in a run of 9.60/160.71. This same car was the first funny car to surpass the 180-mile-per-hour barrier.

Another injected 426 Hemi was guided down the straight and narrow by Ronnie Sox, his 1966 Barracuda sporting a lengthened front end. The Sox & Martin entry was seriously fast, as evidenced by the race against Phil Bonner's Mustang funny car, also graced with a stretched nose. Sox took home a timing slip that recorded an 8.72/167.59. When the second-generation Barracuda was released, it did not take long for the fish to find the strip. One of the first to lunge off the line was Butch Leal in his injected 426 Hemi. Another second-generation Barracuda that found the finish line before the competition was Lime Fire, a 1968 Barracuda that hid

At the 1970 Trans-Am race at Riverside, Dan Gurney led teammate Swede Savage in typically close racing. The race series provided the fans with some of the best racing in years. Notice that the strobe stripe fitted down the side of street 'Cuda AARs was missing from the race cars. With the tendency to change the contour of body panels in racing, it was easier for the crews to get the car's track ready. *Author collection*

The scene, the 1970 Winternationals at the Pomona drag strip. A 1968 Hemi Barracuda Super Stock uses its massive 426-ci engine to rush toward the finish line. This vehicle is properly set up, the body lifting evenly as the wrinkle-walls take a bite and transform the engine's rotational energy into a low elapsed time. *Author collection*

From the painted-on grille to the drag chute, Don "The Snake" Prudhomme's Barracuda Funny Car oozes menace. This car ran during the 1974 season in these colors and was equipped with a Pink-built blown Hemi engine. When it ran the 1973 season, it was sponsored by Carefree gum and won the Nationals by beating Ed "The Ace" McCulloch with a run of 6.38 seconds, tripping the finish line lights at 229.69 miles per hour. *Robert Genat/Zone Five Photo*

an injected 1958 Hemi engine under the one-piece body. That same year, Tom Hoover at Chrysler cajoled a 426 Hemi between the front wheels of a 1968 Barracuda. Then it was made available to the public through select dealers. The result: the Hemi Barracuda Super Stock, spitting out speeds in excess of 130 miles per hour in under 11 seconds. Those were the days!

When the E-body was released in 1970, it was clear this platform had the potential to be blindingly fast in the quarter-mile. With an engine compartment that would comfortably hold any engine in the Chrysler catalog, it did-n't take long before the long-nose, short-deck of the Mopars was found in the staging lights. Ronnie Sox, "Mr. Four-Speed," flew down the quarter in the factory team Hemi 'Cuda in 10.02/137.77 miles per hour at the 1970 Spring Nationals Pro Stock competition. Dick Landy, who knows a thing or two about Hemi engines, campaigned a Challenger car in the door-slammer class. His Hemi engine sported dual-plug heads and a pair of distributors for maximum fuel charge burn. *The Motown Missile*, driven by Don Carlton, like Landy's car, used a twin-plug configuration, and as per the order form it was "to be used as a basis for building the Dept. 1277 automatic transmission test and development car." At the NHRA Grandnationals in Canada, the 1970 Challenger cut a run with a 9.48 elapsed time. Later in the car's life, it was fitted with a four-speed manual transmission.

Plymouth even had a traveling road show in 1970, the Supercar Clinics. Owners of high-performance Plymouths could listen to Ronnie Sox and Buddy Martin talk about what parts were available and tips on how to extract the most power. Set at dealerships, the clinics allowed the racers and Chrysler engineers to explain, face to face, that "you are really getting the hot stuff-no secrets barred. Let's face it-we want you to win!" With a stage full of goodies, the pros had the attention of weekend warriors looking for a few tenths of a second.

The Funny Car ranks were no stranger to the E-body, with vehicles like Gene Snow's Rambunctious Challenger and Don "The Snake" Prudhomme driving the Mattel-sponsored Hemi Funny Car in the 1970 season. Hot Wheels indeed! The John Buttera-built, 1,900-pound 'Cuda was a favorite on the drag circuit. The Ramchargers used a variety of Mopar products, and in 1970, the Dodge, built by Woody Gilmore, was the first Funny Car to run in the 6-second range, with driver Leroy Goldstein pulling a 6.90/211-mile-per-hour run. Another crowd pleaser was the Funny Car 'Cuda of Ed McCulloch, who beat the Mickey Thompson Pinto with a run of 6.64/223.22 miles per hour at the 1971 NHRA Nationals. Mr. Norm, of Grand Spaulding Dodge, put Gary Dyer behind the wheel of the Super Challenger. And Roger Lindamood, who had been a Chrysler Racing Division test driver in the Ramchargers and the Golden Commandos, went his own way in 1966, campaigning a long list of *Color Me Gone* race cars, including a 1971 Challenger.

The Barracuda/Challenger has remained a popular car to run in the quarter-mile. Availability of parts, a wealth of knowledge, and flat-out good looks will keep the Mopar pony cars alive and well, a quarter-mile at a time.

When it came to raising the profile of the Barracuda/Challenger, few could argue with the fact that drag racing has very high visibility. But the road is not always straight. Since the early 1960s, a number of individuals raced the A-body on road courses and rallies with no small amount of success. This in turn would pave the way for Chrysler to enter the high-dollar arena of Trans-Am racing in 1970. Unlike the vehicles that competed at the drag strip in 1,320 foot increments, SCCA Trans-Am and rally race cars were production-based automobiles. And especially in the Trans-Am series, like the E-bodies, it was a story of too little too late.

International Rally Racing

The Plymouth Valiant rally car made its first mark in racing at, of all places, Monaco. But that is where three of the compacts were at the end of the 1964 Monte Carlo Rally. Chrysler sent them overseas to highlight the new 273-ci engine. Chrysler engineer Scott Harvey had competed in rallies previously, so his employer tapped him to lead the race effort in the old country. V-8 engine development and testing was being conducted while the Valiants were being prepared for the race. Six-cylinder engines were installed, so the installation of lead weights was necessary

With Don Grotheer at the wheel, this 1970 'Cuda picks up and flies down the Pomona quarter-mile during the 1970 Winternationals. E-bodies continue to be popular on the drag strip to this day. *Author collection*

to bring the front-end weight to the level of the V-8 engine. Equipped with Goodyear Blue Streak tires, a quicker 16:1 steering gear, bigger front torsion bars, and disc brakes from Girling helped the Valiants tackle the famed off- and on-road race. When the checkered flag flew, Harvey had taken a third in the G. T. class, very respectable indeed. Harvey campaigned all three of the race cars after returning to the United States. He promptly turned one of them into a road-racing car.

When the 1964 Barracuda made its debut, Harvey transferred knowledge learned on the Valiant to the Barracuda. This was the basis for the Formula S package. The success he achieved with the race car was such that Plymouth used Harvey and his race car in a number of advertisements. In the 1965 SCCA season, he was tied for the championship going into the last race with Jerry Titus, who was campaigning a Dart. Titus won the race, Harvey

came in second, and Ford won the Manufacturer's Championship.

During Trans-Am's inaugural season in 1966, Scott Harvey and driver Charlie Rainville ran Barracudas with official factory support under the Team Starfish banner. The team was crewed by Chrysler engineers that took vacation time to turn wrenches. By season's end, the team and its acid-dipped Barracudas had earned second place in the 1966 Trans-American Sedan Racing Manufacturer's Championship. It was an impressive performance from the fledgling team. Thought was given toward building a Corvette Grand Sport fighter for the 1967 season, complete with independent rear suspension, lightened body, and the engine moved rearward, but funds got tight, so the program was axed.

Engine rules did not allow the Barracudas to be competitive in Trans-Am until 1970, but the Barracuda was still fighting for the checkered. Scott Harvey returned to his first love, rally

The most famous Barracuda drag car ever built, the *Hemi Under Glass* was a collaboration between Chrysler and Hurst. With the 426 Hemi engine located behind the driver under the huge rear window, the vehicle would roar down the entire length of the strip on its rear tires alone. First driven by Bill Shrewsberry, it was later piloted by Bob Riggle, who continues to campaign the car today. *Mark Bruederle Photo/Bob Riggle Collection*

Scott Harvey built this exact copy of his 1968 shell 4000 Trans-Canada rally-winning 1967 Barracuda. Driven at the 30th anniversary of the famous run, this vehicle is full of the mechanical tweaks that Harvey incorporated into the original race car, and later became the basis for the Formula S package that turned the Barracuda into an able road machine.

driving, competing in the grueling 1967 Vancouver-to-Montreal rally with a Barracuda. He finished second in this 4,000-mile competition, a warm-up for the 1968 Shell 4000 Trans-Canada rally. With Scott Harvey driving and Ralph Beckman navigating, they took an emotional overall win with their 1967 Barracuda.

Trans-Am, Full Factory Feud

The engine rules in the SCCA's Trans-Am series changed for the 1970 season, allowing manufacturers to adjust the bore and stroke of their production engine to fit the maximum allowed displacement of 305 ci. The 340-ci engine was the basis for the racing engine, but smaller cylinders were fitted to the block in order to conform to the rules. The required size was reached with a bore of 4.040 and a 2.960 stroke for a displacement of 303.8 ci. Before this season, multiple carburetors had been allowed, but revised rules only allowed a single four-barrel carb. Chrysler decided to field entries with both the Barracuda and the new-for-1970 Dodge Challenger. Five factory race cars were built, three Barracudas and two Challengers. Dan Gurney's AAR was tapped to prepare and race the Barracudas, while the Challenger effort was run by Autodynamics Inc.

of Marblehead, Massachusetts. The two car AAR team recruited the driving talents of Dan Gurney and Swede Savage. Sam Posey was the wheelman in the Challenger.

The engines were prepped by famed builder Keith Black. The crankshaft was billet 4340 forged-steel and cross-drilled and the main bearing caps were affixed with four bolts. The heads were massaged 340 units, while a Holley four-barrel sat on an Edelbrock aluminum intake manifold. This combination of parts helped deliver in the neighborhood of 460 horsepower. In the chassis department, Posey's Challenger was outfitted with a special Watts-link rear suspension, while the AARs used the solid rear axle with a panhard rod for lateral location.

The season opener at Laguna Seca was an eye-opener. The Challenger's SubLime green paint stood out in the crowd of competing cars. The AAR cars were painted "New Gurney Blue," a specially mixed hue. The competition was tough, including the Ford Mustang Boss 302s driven by Parnelli Jones and George Follmer, the Chevrolet Z/28s of Jim Hall, and Roger Penske's Javelins, driven by Mark Donohue and Peter Revson.

The Challenger left a lasting impression on its driver. When Posey first got into the Challenger, he was taken by the size. "I had driven a lot of open-wheeled cars, and had done well in sport sedans. But that Challenger was really wide! It looked about a mile wide from the inside, and on the track, when I would get the car a bit sideways, I'd block the whole track."

The acid-dipped body posed a bit of a problem. Seems it had overstayed its visit in the big tank, and the body panels were little more than painted foil. When the tech inspector leaned against the roof, it buckled, sending the crew to a local dealership to cut the roof panel off a new Challenger. But the welded-in roof did little to stiffen the structure. Posey recalled, "I was going through the Corkscrew, watching the ground flash by through the cracks in the floor." Still, he finished sixth and the AAR 'Cuda collected fourth.

As the season wore on, the Challenger team continually fought the chassis, while the AARs just fought the competition. The highlight of the 1970 season, at least for the gang from Chrysler, was the race at Road America. The cars were dialed in on a track that suited the big E-body chassis, and the team was blessed with perfect weather. However, victory was not in the cards, as brake maladies took the cars out of contention. Even with these hurdles, Savage finished second and Posey brought the Challenger T/A across in third. It was the Mopar pony car's finest moment. A third-place finish at Kent and Lime Rock by Posey showed the potential that was in the vehicle, but the program stalled before it got off the ground. Eventually, the two Chrysler teams ended up competing against each other for the 1971 season contract. But that was not to be.

The end of the 1970 season saw Chrysler pull out of the Trans-Am series. Posey said, "We were really hurt. We had busted our asses in that first season, and we knew that the next year would see us winning." The world was changing and along with it, the automotive market. Musclecars had reached their crescendo, and the inevitable decline would soon follow. The racing program was deemed too costly, so Chrysler pulled the plug. Ford and Chevrolet had pulled out of the Trans-Am as well.

But this was not the last time that a Challenger took to a race track with curves. A convertible Dodge Challenger was the pace car for the 1971 Indianapolis 500 race. A group of local Dodge dealers got together and agreed to supply the brickyard with a pace car and backup. Painted Hemi-Orange with a white interior, it was a head turner. The profile of the E-body would be seen in 1,320-foot increments from then on, signaling the demise of Mopar Pony Car performance on road courses. But it had been a good run.

INDEX